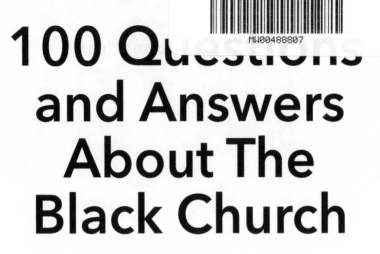

100 Questions and Answers About The Black Church

The Social and Spiritual Movement of a People

**Michigan State University
School of Journalism**

Front Edge Publishing

For more information and further discussion, visit

news.jrn.msu.edu/culturalcompetence/

ISBN: 978-1-64180-155-3

Version 1.0

Cover design and illustration by Rick Nease

www.RickNeaseArt.com

Published by

Front Edge Publishing

42807 Ford Road, No. 234

Canton, MI, 48187

Front Edge Publishing books are available for discount bulk purchases for events, corporate use and small groups. Special editions, including books with corporate logos, personalized covers and customized interiors, are available for purchase. For more information, contact Front Edge Publishing at info@FrontEdgePublishing.com.

Contents

The authors of this guide with leaders at St. Stephen's Community Church in Lansing, Michigan. From left, front row: Pastor Rev. Sameerah L. Shareef, Jaden Beard, Payton Wells and Gabby Neufeld. Second row from left: Cameron Harp, London Asbury, Isabelle Jenkins, Angela Solomon and Amanda VanJaarsveld. Third row from left: Devin Crawford, Associate Pastor Rev. Charles Corley, Leslie Nguyen, Karly Graham, Nyla Kennedy and Mark Krueger-VanOyen. Also: Sydney Bowler and Luke Czach. Lacie Kunselman helped edit and produce this guide.

Acknowledgments

We thank the people at St. Stephen's Community Church in Lansing, Michigan, and Hartford Memorial Baptist Church in Detroit for welcoming us. We also interviewed many people to decide which questions should go into the guide. We are grateful for allies who critiqued those questions and drafts for accuracy and tone. Major allies include:

The **Rev. Sameerah L. Shareef** is senior pastor of St. Stephen's Community Church, United Church of Christ, in Lansing, Michigan. She has worked her way up since 1996 serving as a deacon, youth minister, girls' rites of passage director, women's minister, associate pastor, assistant pastor and transition pastor. Shareef earned a bachelor's degree from Michigan State University, a master's in nursing from Case Western Reserve University and a master's of divinity from Chicago Theological Seminary.

The **Rev. Charles Corley** works with Shareef as associate pastor and outreach community developer at St. Stephen's Community Church, which he joined in 1993. He has been a deacon and became a licensed minister and member of the St. Stephen's ministerial team in 2003. Corley has been chairperson of the board of directors of the Michigan Conference of the United Church of Christ. He is on the criminal justice faculty at Michigan State University. He earned a bachelor's degree at Hampton Institute, and master's and doctorate degrees from Bowling Green State University.

Bobbi Bowman is a career journalist by profession and a historian by avocation. She has been the diversity director for the American Society of News Editors and an editor at The Washington Post, the Detroit Free Press and the Utica Observer Dispatch in New York. Bowman was inducted into the National Association of Black Journalists' Hall of Fame as part of the Metro Seven. In 1972, the group filed a formal complaint with the U.S. Equal Employment Opportunity Commission over Post hiring practices. She earned a bachelor's degree in history from Albright University and a master's in urban affairs from American University.

The **Rev. Robert Jones** is described by photographer James Fraher as, "Perhaps the world's most highly educated blues musician, an ordained minister, a longtime DJ, and a living encyclopedia of blues history, the Rev. Robert Jones is comfortable among juke joint loud talkers, fancy-hatted church ladies, and PhDs alike." Jones, of Detroit, performs throughout the United States, Canada and Europe. He is the former host of the award-winning radio programs "Blues from the Lowlands" and "Deep River" broadcast on Detroit Public Radio's WDET-FM Detroit. He has taught music history courses at Wayne State University in Detroit.

Dr. Terri Laws is an associate professor of African and African American Studies at the University of Michigan-Dearborn. She earned a PhD in Religious Studies with a concentration in African American Religions at Rice University. Areas of interest include race, religion, and society with healthcare and health inequities. Her teaching and research agenda includes the African American religious experience, medical ethics, Black and Womanist religious thought, and introduction to African American Studies. She is co-chair of the Bioethics and Religion Unit of the American Academy of Religion and a member of the Society for the Study of Black Religion.

Dr. Deborah Smith Pollard is a professor at the University of Michigan-Dearborn. Her interests include African and African American studies, English, humanities, women's & gender studies. She is author of "When the Church Becomes Your Party: Contemporary Gospel Music." Plus, she blogs and has had a gospel music program on Detroit's WJLB-FM 98 since 1994. She was named Gospel Announcer of the Year in the Stellar Awards, gospel music's equivalent to the Grammys. For many years she co-produced the McDonald's Gospelfest and the Motor City Praisefest in Detroit. Pollard earned her doctorate from Michigan State University where her focus was American Studies. She earned her master's degree at Wayne State University.

Dr. Marisa A. Smith is an assistant professor in Michigan State University's Department of Advertising + Public Relations and its School of Journalism. Smith's research investigates news disseminated in digital environments and the sociopolitical influence of these messages. She earned her doctorate in communication from the University of Illinois at Urbana-Champaign.

As we often do in this series, we relied on the work of the Pew Research Center. Its most recent study on this subject has been "Faith Among Black Americans," a subject of Pew's continuing study. The Interfaith Leadership Council of Metropolitan Detroit also advised.

Our text was "The Black Church: This Is Our Story, This Is Our Song," by **Henry Louis Gates Jr.** We referred to it frequently and highly recommend it and the PBS documentary by the same name as a next step for our readers.

This guide and its related projects are supported by grants from Michigan State University's Office for Institutional Diversity and Inclusion, The College of Communication Arts and Sciences and the School of Journalism. The principal figures in those groups are, respectively, Vice President and Chief Diversity Officer **Jabbar R. Bennett**, Dean **Prabu David** and Director **Tim Vos**.

Foreword

"No pillar of the African American community has been more central to its history, identity and social justice vision than the Black Church."

Henry Louis Gates Jr.

By Freda G. Sampson

I am the answered prayer and product of the Black Church!

I am the granddaughter, daughter, sister, niece, cousin and friend of preachers, theologians and academic portals of divinity. I am not a preacher, but I am one of the many voices of the Black Church. I am her biggest fan and sometimes most vocal critic. I personally know the impact of the church on its people, its communities, and their social, political and economic development.

I grew up in the church, my father was a pastor and, as it is with most PKs (preachers' kids), from infancy to adolescence and through adulthood, I spent a lot of time within the walls of the church. It is here that I learned the difference between doing "church work" and "the work of the church." I learned so many of life's lessons from the Black Church. My first and only singing solo, my first public speaking welcoming the visitors on Sunday morning, my first community engagement and organizing to combat gang activity in the neighborhood, my first heartbreak, my first experience of death, and occasionally my trust in others being broken. These experiences have shaped me and shook me to awaken to the fact that prayer and action are faith requirements to fight against injustice and for humanity.

In the Black Church, I have seen the jubilation of faith expressed in ways that celebrate life and yet examine the pain of racism, sexism, patriarchy, oppression, classism, ageism and bias against sexual orientation. It is conservative, liberal, large, small and mega. It grapples with "isms" and identities, and it gives volumes to people whose voices have been marginalized.

The Black Church has been and continues to be a visible and invisible institution that profoundly influences the spiritual and social lives of its people. It is a holy foundation, a sanctuary of faith and a center of liberation. As a term, it is both singular and plural. It can represent one congregation, or it can represent the totality of Black Churches, denominations and conventions. It is a religious collection of prayers, songs, preaching and service to God through our service to others. It is the incubator that provides experiences for our children to flourish. The Black Church is LIFE!

The culture of the Black Church is inclusive of both the spoken and the sung word from the brilliant minds, diverse perspectives and oratorical art of the preacher to the music in the songs of spirituals and gospel and its influences on genres of music from jazz and blues, to hip-hop. W. E. B. Du Bois, American sociologist, historian, scholar and author of "The Souls of Black Folk: Essays and Sketches" wrote in 1903 about the preacher, the music and the frenzy. Categorically, these aspects are profoundly important, but there is more that embodies the Black Church in depth and in substance. Hundreds of others have continued to tell of the rich experience of the Black Church through rigorous scholarship and historical context.

This guide focuses on the Black Church through the lens of the Christian religion. It does not suggest that other faith traditions do or do not refer to themselves in this manner, and it is not to exclude other faith traditions that have members who are African American. This guide is a window to learn more about an institution which has had a significant impact on the American experiment.

I am thrilled about this project and proud of the students that took on this work. I am grateful for the leaders and scholars that reviewed the content and offered their voices to assure that the information is accurate. As with other guides in the series, it provides an opportunity to be curious and learn of some nuances that make up the Black Church experience. My hope is the questions asked and answered will give you insight and connect you to an ongoing movement that is a critical part of the spiritual and social voice of a people and an institution that in the words of my father, Rev. Dr Frederick G Sampson II, has informed this nation that justice looks like love in action.

The editor of this guide is Freda G. Sampson. She is committed to bridging racial and cultural divisions through community engagement, advocacy and organizational development. She has implemented diversity, equity and inclusion in nonprofit and corporate organizations. Sampson has been project manager for the Michigan Roundtable for Diversity and Inclusion. Sampson's entrepreneurial ventures have  *included owning several coffee houses in Detroit. Sampson has a master's of fine arts from the University of Michigan, a bachelor of arts in communication from Tennessee State University and an associate of arts degree from Brooks School of Design in Long Beach, California. In 2016, she received certification as a qualified administrator for intercultural development. Leadership courses have included New Detroit's Multicultural Leadership Program, Harvard University's School of Divinity Leadership Program and the University of Michigan's Worldview Seminar on World Religions.*

Introduction

By The Rev. Charles Christian Adams

The Black Church and the African American worship experience has been an all-encompassing endeavor. It looms large in the world, especially in the lives of those whose ancestors were once a part of the "peculiar institution" of chattel slavery in America. Once an expression that was outlawed, along with literacy, for the enslaved, the church has become the center of their existence. Its leaders have changed the world for the better and helped humanity to morally progress in labor relations, distribution of resources, education, health care, equal protection under the law, access to opportunity, housing, economic development and social activism. Although everyone does not belong to the Black Church, the Black Church belongs to everybody. This tradition has never had the luxury of being exclusively concerned with ecclesiastical machinations or sacerdotal exercise. Its relevance has permeated all aspects of life. Once, when speaking at the Morehouse College baccalaureate service in 1995, my pastor for 48 years said in the prose of preaching:

> "The Black Church is the producer of our genius
> the guarantor of our sanity
> the power base for our political ascendancy
> the parent of our music and art
> the sponsor of our creativity
> the incubator of our leadership
> the storehouse for the disinherited
> a hospital for wounded souls
> a love tabernacle for the hated and exploited
> and an open door to the least, the last, the little, the
> unlucky and the left out."

A question that flows as a transit of logic could be, "How do we access this power?" This is why this quick reference is so important. It is to all who will take advantage of it a great resource to connect with a community and culture. We celebrate diversity when we are at our best. However, you can't glean from this field of dreams if you don't know the specifics and have at least a perfunctory knowledge of what you behold. It is just enough information and history to let you know how it all works. One of my doctoral professors remarked that in academia and other disciplines, the "lived experience" has taken a new significance. This reading is concise but in no way superfluous. So when you encounter the efficacy of the African American worship tradition or if you seek it out, you will be well prepared. Even if you just want to know enough to increase your understanding, you will enjoy this offering.

The church I pastor is on the northwest side of Detroit. This is one of the most economically challenged areas in the city, although there are many stable homes within its parameters. It is predominately African American. Out of that pathos has emerged such a generosity and greatness of soul and spirit that it is truly a blessed enterprise. One Sunday, two of our White brothers came to our service and said to one of our ushers that they really wanted to hear an African American choir live. She said, "You're in the right place!" When the gentlemen left, I think one of them was saying, "Surely the Lord is in this place!"

The Rev. Charles Christian Adams is pastor of Hartford Memorial Baptist Church in Detroit, where he was ordained under the pastorate of his father, Dr. Charles G. Adams. The Rev. Adams earned his bachelor of arts degree from Wayne State University in Detroit, and his master's of divinity degree from Union Theological  *Seminary of New York City. The Rev. Adams preaches and teaches monthly at Ryan Correctional Facility, is a member of the Golden Key National Honor Society and a lifetime member of the NAACP. He serves on the board of directors for the Detroit Recovery Project and The Emmanuel House Recovery Center. He is also on the board for Loyola High School, the advisory board for the American Baptist Women in Ministry and St. Jude Research Hospital. He is board president of The Metropolitan Christian Council of Detroit and Windsor.*

Preface

The 2021 book and PBS documentary "The Black Church: This Is Our Story, This Is Our Song," prompted us to create this guide.

The Black Church had been on our list for this series. Henry Louis Gates Jr.'s book and the documentary, as well as the reception they received, gave us the push to publish.

The Black Church is a unique American institution with its own formation and structure. People have a lot of questions about it. Subjects like this are our niche for this series of more than 20 guides.

The Bias Busters series tries to answer the most basic, entry-level questions people have about each other. We believe most people want to learn but might worry their questions will come off wrong or hurt someone. They worry their questions might make them seem ignorant. Or they just don't know anyone to ask.

We try to give them a safe start.

Students in a journalism class at Michigan State University asked people familiar with the Black Church to tell us basic questions people have about the church. What questions do they hear? What misconceptions? We gathered the questions and then went after the research and authoritative sources for answers.

One hundred questions cannot tell the whole story. One thousand questions won't, either. The more you ask, the more you learn, and the more questions you have.

There is another dimension to this. The Black Church, like all groups of people, holds incredible diversity within itself. As an array of seven independent denominations with thousands of churches that choose their own leaders, there are no one-size-fits-all answers.

Even people who go to the same house of worship or live in the same place see things differently. In class, we say, "Once you know what one person thinks, you know what exactly one person thinks." What is true for one is not true for all. As you continue your research, we encourage you to ask a number of people the same questions to get the full picture.

We hope this guide helps you talk to friends and acquaintances who know the Black Church. We hope you read more about Black Churches and visit some, where you will be welcomed.

With an article about Gates' projects, TIME magazine published the headline, "To understand America, you need to understand the Black Church."

We agree. Learning about each other teaches us about ourselves. We have found that the more we learn about each other, the more we see how similar we are, united by the same issues and hopes.

Enjoy your adventure.

Joe Grimm
Series editor
Bias Busters
Michigan State University School of Journalism

Identity

1 What is the Black Church?

The Black Church is a group of Protestant churches created in response to segregation and discrimination. It has several denominations. The Black Church is not just physical places. The church is a spiritual and social institution. Black Churches are pillars of Black communities. The church has been and continues to be a haven for people to be validated, protected and spiritually renewed. The institution has long been and continues to be a leader in theology and social justice movements including advances in civil and voting rights. It protects and promotes Black culture and power.

2 What are the denominations?

Some have called the "The Black Church" sociological shorthand that envelopes several primary denominations. The largest is the National Baptist Convention, USA. It has roughly 8.43 million members across 21,000 congregations. Here are the churches frequently classified as Black Churches, in the order they were founded.

1816: African Methodist Episcopal Church

1821: African Methodist Episcopal Zion Church

1870: Christian Methodist Episcopal Church

1880: National Baptist Convention, USA, Inc.

1897: Church of God in Christ

1915: National Baptist Convention of America International, Inc.

1961: Progressive National Baptist Convention, Inc.

3 Why were Black Churches created?

Slavery and segregation provoked the creation of independent churches that grew out of Protestant churches. Many enslaved people were members of those churches but only to a limited extent. The churches often taught a distorted version of Christianity to justify slavery. Black people were compelled to create their own churches. There, they were free to gather, worship and learn. In these churches, they were able to exercise leadership and blend Christianity and African traditions. Besides their Christian faith, members prioritized social, economic and political service.

4 What is the role of the Black Church today?

The bedrock values continue to play a foundational role in today's Black Church. While the values have not changed, contemporary circumstances change the way people act on those values. Two examples are more intense political organizing and alignment with the Black Lives Matter movement.

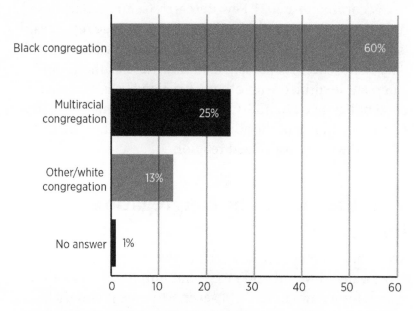

Percent of congregations Black Americans attend

Of Black Americans who attend religious services, a majority attend Black congregations.

- Black congregation — 60%
- Multiracial congregation — 25%
- Other/white congregation — 13%
- No answer — 1%

Source: Pew Research Center and World Religion Database   Graphic by Karly Graham

5 Are all majority African American churches "Black Churches?"

No. The racial makeup of the congregation does not determine whether an institution is a Black Church. The designation is based on values and history. Some newer majority Black Christian churches do not share the history or Black Churches' emphasis on social issues.

6 Do African Americans belong to other churches?

Yes, according to a 2021 Pew Research Center report based on a survey of 8,660 Black adults. The 176-page report said two-thirds of Black Americans are Protestant. Most attend Black Churches. Six percent said they were Catholic, and 3 percent identified with other Christian faiths. Another 3 percent belonged to non-Christian faiths, primarily Islam. About one in five of the adults surveyed said they are not affiliated with an organized religion.

7 Is the race of the congregation important?

According to that Pew Research report, 63 percent of Black Americans surveyed said race is not important when they search for a new church. However, 61 percent said their congregations should diversify racially and ethnically. Some Black Churches have non-Black pastors, just as some mostly White or multi-ethnic churches have Black pastors.

Arrival

8 Did enslaved people arrive as Christians?

No. Most people brought in captivity from Africa to the Americas held a variety of beliefs and practices. Many belonged to traditional African religions. Some were Muslim. However, in the Americas, traditional beliefs were discouraged, and people were persecuted for practicing them. Many sought something to believe in.

9 Why did enslaved people convert to Christianity?

Some Methodist and Baptist enslavers forced people to convert. They believed their own salvation could come from winning converts and that converting would make people in bondage more compliant. Some Black people sought membership in Christian churches to move up the social ladder. Many Black converts identified with Jesus, his plight and his promise of deliverance.

10 Could enslaved people read the Bible?

Education was seen as a threat to a social and economic system based on forced labor. Between 1740 and 1834, most Southern states enacted anti-literacy laws. It became illegal to teach Black people to read or write. Those who broke the law by teaching literacy could be fined, jailed or whipped. Some enslaved people suspected of literacy were beaten or had fingers or toes amputated. However, some enslavers believed Christianity could be used to control the enslaved. Some used the Bible to encourage that, and a "Slave Bible" was published.

11 What was the "Slave Bible"?

This was used to expose enslaved people to Christianity. It was a shorter, distorted version of the Bible. Chapters that seemed to condone rebellion or hope, such as the Book of Exodus, were cut. Books that mentioned slavery, such as Leviticus, were kept. Anthony Schmidt, an associate curator at the Museum of the Bible in Washington, D.C., told National Public Radio, "About 90 percent of the Old Testament is missing (and) 50 percent of the New Testament is missing." These Bibles were first published in London in 1807. They were used primarily in the Caribbean Islands and were not in widespread use. It is unclear how many copies were published. Three are known to exist today.

12 Could enslaved people practice Christianity openly?

Most were not allowed to practice Christianity openly on their own, so many practiced in secret. Historians have referred to the early Black Church as "The Invisible Institution." African Americans often hid their meetings for fear of being punished or beaten.

13 Did enslavers discourage individual prayer?

Many did. However, religion is very personal to Black people. They would call out to the Lord at all times of the day wherever they were. So, personal prayer went on, often undetected. Some enslavers feared group prayer and tried to suppress it. Others thought their churches, which remained segregated, could be used to justify slavery. Enslaved people sought refuge in small buildings and clearings where they could develop their own religion. These secret places were called "hush harbors" and "praise houses." Many meetings happened on weeknights. Where organized religion was forbidden, enslaved people whispered their prayers into basins or pots called "prayer kettles" so they would not be caught.

Origins

14 When did the Black Church start?

Denominations were created at different times. Most began
as single churches. The first organized Black Church was a
Baptist house, started by the Rev. George Liele in Savannah
in 1773. This precedes the official formation of the United
States in 1776.

15 What drove Black people to form actual churches?

White people did not allow Black people to have equal
status in White churches. A stark example occurred in
Philadelphia in 1787. Sociologist and historian W. E. B.
Du Bois wrote that Black congregants, who had been
segregated at St. George's Methodist Church, formed the
nondenominational Free African Society.

16 Was the Free African Society a church?

Not at first. Preachers Richard Allen, Absalom Jones and
other Black founders intended to build a Christian church
that reflected African heritage and responded to racism

in majority White churches. However, Black churches were discouraged. So, the society instead provided schools, burial space, economic and emotional support to recently freed Africans.

17 What led the society to form a church?

Continued segregation in worship actually led to two Black Churches. As St. George's Methodist expanded, it maintained a color line. Black leaders helped expand the church, but were required to sit out of sight in the balcony. In 1792, some Black members were forced out of the church for sitting in pews not designated for them. They did not come back. They formed St. Thomas' African Episcopal Church and Jones became pastor. Later that year, Allen founded the Bethel African Methodist Episcopal Church.

18 How did African religious traditions influence the Black Church?

There are several similarities between the Black Church and traditional African religions. The church is a melding of African, European, and African American cultural and religious traditions. Many practices of the Black Church stemmed from African influences, including the importance of baptism, music and song.

19 What are fundamental beliefs of the Black Church?

Their primary texts are the Old and New Testaments. They profess belief in God, whose son is Jesus, and the Holy Spirit. Many believe God is necessary for a person to have good morals and values. Beyond these core beliefs, there is variety. There are different approaches to how the Bible should be interpreted and who should do that. Many believe God influences what is happening in the world and determines what will happen in our lives. Many pray daily. Some trust this can heal illness or injury. Some believe evil spirits can harm people.

20 How are Black Churches different from other Protestant churches?

Black Churches emphasize liberation, affirmation and social issues. They more frequently address social needs. According to Pew research, around three-quarters of Black adults say predominantly Black Churches have helped Black people in the United States move toward equality "a great deal" (29 percent) or "some" (48 percent). Members count on the church for spiritual comfort, community, moral guidance, help with bills, housing and food, job and life skills as well as racial affirmation.

21 How important is the social mission?

The social mission is crucial. It is the major factor that distinguished the Black Church from other Protestant denominations. Social values do not merely accompany the spiritual. The two reinforce one another. Without either one, the Black Church would lose much of its identity.

22 What characterizes a Black Church service?

Jesus Christ remains central to the service, and there are unique cultural differences in sermons and praise. Compared to other Protestant services, sermons in Black Churches much more frequently deal with Christ-centered aspects of issues such as race relations, equity and prison reform. Sermons or homilies have a formal structure. Many preachers practice the art of homiletics, the application of rhetorical techniques to theology. Often, this means a topic introduction, a three-point body on the topic and a summary. Sermons or homilies are written and delivered to inspire and exhort the congregation. Responses by congregants to the preacher's call show that the message has been received. Music and praise are important elements throughout. A music team, instruments and sound systems help carry the service.

Great Awakenings

23 How did Christian reforms affect Americans?

There have been several Christian revival movements in the United States. The First Great Awakening rolled across Britain and the American colonies in 1730-1790. Evangelical Protestant revivalists wanted new enthusiasm for religion and rejected state religions. They sought more egalitarian churches. New churches were formed, and non-ordained men became pastors. African Americans began joining Christianity in large numbers.

24 What happened in the next awakening?

The Second Great Awakening (1790-1840) gave rise to evangelicalism and emphasized people's ability to improve their lives through their own free will. It taught that Christ's salvation was available to all people. The role of White women in religion grew, as did African-American participation in Christianity. Churches, especially in the North, worked for the abolition of slavery.

25 How were Black Churches in particular affected?

The awakenings brought the Bible to many more Black people. This fostered a culturally relevant relationship with Christianity. The Second Great Awakening led to many new independent churches in the United States. Many Americans abandoned the concept of hierarchical churches in favor of churches that promoted spiritual equality. African Americans established independent churches.

Demographics

26 How large is the Black Church?

About two-thirds of Black American adults identify as Protestants, and most of them attend Black Churches. The Census Bureau reported there were 41.1 million Black people of all ages in the United States in 2020. This would put membership across Black Churches in the tens of millions.

27 Where is the church most prevalent today?

According to Pew, the highest participation in the Black Church is in the South. There, 65 percent of Black adults who estimate they go to church at least a few times a year say they go to a Black Church. The Midwest is next at 60 percent. It is followed by 52 percent in the Northeast and 38 percent in the West.

28 Did southern and northern churches differ?

The Black Church has always been multi-denominational, so differences are natural. Black Churches began in the

South as well as the North, where free and enslaved Blacks all experienced segregation. They shared beliefs and grievances but developed different styles of worship and praise.

29 How did Black migration to the North affect the church?

From the 1910s to the 1970s, 6 million African Americans moved from the agricultural South to the industrial North. This was the 60-year Great Migration. People relocated for greater opportunities and freedoms. Many found that conditions in the North were not much better than what they had left. They had to work long hours in dangerous and dirty factory jobs. They were confined to segregated, overcrowded areas. Home ownership was denied or discouraged. In the North, people found a religious home and social networks for healthcare and employment in churches. However, many found the worship style to be less infused with African traditions. Some people new to the North saw this as an unwanted compromise to gain social acceptance.

30 Was social acceptance achieved?

In "The Black Church: This Is Our Story, This Is Our Song," Henry Louis Gates Jr. explains this "politics of respectability." He describes how people sought social approval with services that seemed more similar to those in White churches. Michael Eric Dyson, a professor, author and minister, wrote, "respectability politics was born in a good way when Black people were trying to adjust to the new situation for us to win and curry favor morally. But the irony is, we're trying to convince White people to see us as human ... They don't see you as human. Dressing nicely can't do it. Speaking the king's English to the queen's taste is not going to flip the switch."

31 How did the migration change worship?

Storefront churches grew out of the Great Migration as migrants sought spiritual meeting places. Urban storefronts, more abundant than they were in the rural South, were accessible and affordable. Some storefront churches developed detailed and elaborate displays. Some echoed the emotion and storytelling of preaching. Some Black Churches eventually acquired edifices built by other denominations. Eventually, they built their own, including some that became megachurches serving thousands.

Sanctuaries

32 How are Black Churches sanctuaries?

All houses of worship are or have sanctuaries, but the word holds special meaning in the Black Church. From their beginning, these places have been more than houses of worship. They are places to gather safely, find solace and attain positions and respect denied by the outside community. They have been one of the only places that would teach African Americans or provide mutual aid and social services. Dyson has called the Black Church "our refuge. It's our sanctuary, literally. The very nature of the Black Church is what makes it so powerful and yet so vulnerable at the same time."

33 How are Black Churches vulnerable?

Growing visibility brought down racist violence on churches even before the pre-Civil War period, when the Black Church played a role in abolition. Ever since, people have targeted churches to strike at Black communities and oppose civil rights. Yolanda Pierce, an associate professor of African American Religion at Princeton Theological Seminary, said, "The attack is actually on the African American community at large, and the church acts as the symbol for this."

34 Were churches attacked during the civil rights struggle?

There were frequent burnings and bombings at Black Churches during the civil rights movement. In September 1963, four girls, ages 11 to 14, were killed in a Sunday bombing at 16th Street Baptist Church in Birmingham, Alabama. People began calling the city "Bombingham." Copycat attacks in other cities followed, and anonymous callers threatened churches.

35 Are churches still attacked?

In response to a wave of church arsons, Congress in 1996 increased penalties for arson against religious organizations, especially when racially or ethnically motivated. In June 2015, a White supremacist murdered nine people at a Bible study inside Emanuel African Methodist Episcopal Church in Charleston, South Carolina. The killer, who said he hoped to ignite a race war, chose Emanuel because it was one of the oldest Black Churches in the country and a center for civil rights activity. Within the month, according to Baptist Press, seven more Black Churches were burned. Annual FBI crime statistics show that about two-thirds of racially motivated hate crimes in the United States target African Americans. Many are aimed at churches.

Structure

36 Does the Black Church have a hierarchy?

Each denomination has an independent governing structure. At the national or regional level, there are leaders and governing boards or assemblies. Titles vary. They include president, archbishop, presiding bishop and bishop. Leaders are elected and may have terms that expire. Individual congregations are typically led by a pastor who is chosen locally. Larger churches also have associate and assistant pastors, deacons and elders. In some denominations, there are honorific titles acquired by seniority. Not all traditions treat titles the same way. In some churches, a deacon is a clergy person. In others, deacons are elected to terms. Today's Black Church has affiliates and members around the world.

37 What is the preacher's role?

The preacher, who might also be the pastor, leads the congregation in prayer and worship. They are the spiritual leaders of the church. Boards support and oversee the work and finances of the church. Preachers visit the sick and shut in, are leaders in their community and grow the church by "saving souls." Preachers are historically important in African American communities and have led civil rights initiatives. Du Bois wrote, "The preacher is the most unique personality developed by the Negro on American soil. A leader, a politician, an orator, a 'boss,' an intriguer, an idealist — all these he is."

38 How many pastors does a church have?

The larger the church, the more leaders, ministers and general staff it needs and can support. In most churches, the leadership team tends to have one pastor with associate or assistant pastors.

39 What is the minister of music's role?

Many faiths have music directors. In the Black Church, this person is director of both vocal and instrumental praise. This can mean selecting and directing the choir, choosing and leading or directing music and dance, and motivating congregational participation. The minister of music is active beyond church services, arranging concerts and performances. The job description can include planning and implementing a music ministry for the pastor, congregation and community. Choirs often play a major role throughout the week in the facilitation of praise and worship, as well as during offering, before the sermon and during invitation.

40 What is the etiquette for visiting a Black Church?

Expect to be approached and to be welcomed. Dress codes vary according to the church, the region and the type of service. It is best to stay on the Sunday-best side with women in dresses and men in business or business casual, especially on the first Sunday of the month. Some church websites might give you an idea of how people dress. Non-members are welcome to participate. However, just observe communion, healings or altar calls, in which congregants come forward and ask God for help.

Social Mission

41 What is the Black social gospel?

This theology stems from the abolition movement. It sustained the fight for Black rights throughout post-Civil War Reconstruction, passage of the 14th and 15th Amendments, the Jim Crow era, and the Black Lives Matter movement. According to "The New Abolition" by Gary Dorrien, the Black social gospel "describes Martin Luther King Jr., his chief mentors, his best allies, and the entire tradition of Black Church social justice activism."

42 Were Black Churches in the Underground Railroad?

Many accounts describe churches that were stations on the railroad from the South to Canada. Conductors along the secret network hid, fed and clothed people on their journeys to the next station. Sandwich First Baptist Church near Ontario, Canada, is one of many churches with an underground railroad museum documenting its history.

43 What role did the church have in the civil rights movement?

Black Churches were places for African Americans to gather and share strategies. They hosted political discussion, debated, spread awareness about the movement and raised money. Civil rights became an important part of religious preaching in many Black Churches. Many pastors and members led civil rights demonstrations, exposing themselves to violence.

The Rev. Robert Jones offers a musical history of how "We Shall Overcome," the anthem of the civil rights movement, came to be.

Scan the code or visit the link to view: youtu.be/zVIiAkz0XmM

44 Were there similar efforts for voting rights?

Black Church leaders had a large impact on this campaign. Dr. Martin Luther King Jr. founded the Southern Christian Leadership Conference in 1957 to assist local groups fighting for equality. The organization registered voters and supported marches. These contributed to the passage of the Voting Rights Act of 1965. Today, some Black Churches offer rides, food and water on Election Day. They have supported Sunday as a voting day and other reforms and oppose pushback by those trying to restrict voting access in marginalized communities.

45 What is Black Liberation Theology?

The philosophy springs from civil rights activism. The Rev. James Cone, creator of this philosophy, described it on National Public Radio as an effort "to teach people how to be both unapologetically Black and Christian at the same time." This counters centuries of portrayals of Black people as evil. Black Liberation Theology makes Jesus' message relevant to Black people and encourages them to love themselves. It includes the ideas of King and Malcolm X. It can mean envisioning God as Black.

46 What is the church's role in Black Lives Matter?

Many churches support the movement and help members get involved. As with the civil rights era, church members debate strategies. Pastors, ministers and clergy of this and other faiths march to support Black Lives Matter. The idea of churches as sanctuaries and Black Lives Matter intersected in December 2020. Then, White supremacists burned a Black Lives Matter banner taken from historic Asbury United Methodist Church in Washington, D.C. The church soon replaced it.

47 How does the church regard LGBTQ+ people?

This has been described as a "don't ask, don't tell" relationship. Churches have been called the most unwelcoming part of the Black community. But there is a dichotomy. Anti-LGBTQ+ sermons may come from the pulpit, yet the pews and choirs are filled with people of these very identities. Many people have left churches that opposed their identity. Some who stay in the church feel they must hide their identities.

48 Is the stance toward LGBTQ+ people changing?

The Human Rights Campaign, an advocacy group, notes some thawing. It expressed hope on its website that, "as more churches open their doors to LGBTQ parishioners and more leaders publicly recognize those of different sexual orientations and gender identities, fewer LGBTQ African Americans will be forced to choose between their identities and their faiths."

Praise

49 How are praise and worship services different from devotional services?

Praise and worship express gratitude and admiration of God. This includes singing, dancing, shouting and praying. Praise and worship may kick off a service and last 15-20 minutes. Devotional services consist of nine processes: hearing, chanting, remembering, serving the Lord, deity worship, praying, carrying out the orders of the world, becoming friends with the Lord, and surrendering everything to him.

50 What is the worship style in Black Churches?

There is a range from quiet and conservative to expressive. In most churches, some congregants call out "amen" or other affirming responses during sermons. In more expressive churches, people will also shout, cry out, run or dance. Worship is not confined to services. Studies show that Black Americans would rather rely on God than a religious leader to guide them through life. According to the Pew Research Center, a vast majority of Black Americans pray to God several times a month outside of church. Many said they pray every day.

51 Does shouting "amen" interrupt sermons?

No, calling out is not an interruption. It is participation that affirms the message and the messenger. This is call and response in action. It has variations in preaching, music and dance. Even classroom teachers use it. Call and response was brought to the United States from sub-Saharan Africa. In worship, the preacher typically calls out a question or beckons a response. By responding to the preacher's call, worshipers show they are into the message and the moment, carrying it along. In this tradition, a sermon that draws no responses is not working. The energy and personal involvement attract some people to call-and-response services.

52 What type of preaching occurs in the Black Church?

Styles vary from preacher to preacher. They include a teaching/lecture style, storytelling, to hooping and more often than not, a combination of two or more. "Hooping," also called whooping, is an exuberant style of preaching that some Black preachers use in their sermons. It involves speaking loudly and using energetic movements to engage with the congregation. When the preacher is "hooping," congregants will often respond to show they agree with the message.

53 Why are movement, energy and emotion important to praise?

Movement, energy and emotion elevate praise. Showing energy implies one is excited and eager to show gratitude and recognition. Expressing emotion is both an outlet for expressing generational trauma and opening oneself to a better relationship with God. When spiritual, intellectual and physical experiences come together during worship, it is a sign that the Holy Ghost is present. The New Testament described this phenomenon at Pentecost when the Holy Spirit visited the disciples of Jesus after his ascension.

54 How does dance praise God?

Traditional African cultures used dance to connect their communities and to reach spiritual deities. People would use movement to tell stories of the past and call upon spirits for protection and good harvests. The Bible has multiple examples of people dancing, shouting and leaping in praise. This practice continues in the modern Black Church. The praise dancer is a medium for these cultural movements. Symbolically calling upon God, the dancer embodies elegance and pageantry. Many churches have liturgical dance ministries that animate musical lyrics in Sunday liturgy and create special events.

55 Why do some people raise their hands in worship?

People in many religions pray with their hands in different ways. Some make the sign of the cross, some extend their hands in blessing to others. There is clapping and applauding and some people shake hands to greet each other. In some faiths, hands are laid upon people to heal or ordain them. Ushers use gestures to communicate with each other wordlessly across the church. As preachers in many religions demonstrate, hands speak loudly. Powerful gestures of beseeching, offering up and making praise have many biblical mentions. Psalm 134:2 says, "Lift up your hands to the holy place and bless the LORD!" People raise their hands to invite the Holy Spirit or to indicate his presence in them. In the Black Church, people may signify they feel God's presence by raising hands or extending them.

56 What is speaking in tongues?

Speaking in tongues means to shout or speak with sounds that are outside of known languages. When someone speaks in tongues, it is an act of praise that means the Holy Ghost has taken control of their speech. The person is said to be speaking directly to God. The technical name for this is glossolalia. This gift of the Holy Spirit happens in Pentecostal and evangelical churches.

57 What does evangelical mean?

It is important to distinguish between evangelizing and being an evangelical Christian. Many faiths evangelize. It means seeking converts to Christianity. For evangelical Protestants, evangelizing is an essential and defining characteristic. While Black Church Christians may evangelize, they are distinct from evangelical Christians. It is the Black Church's role as social and civic institution, not its belief in Christ or evangelizing, that sets it apart.

58 What are other praise traditions?

Praise traditions can range from prayer to hollering, the ring shout, dancing and testifying. The ring shout stems from West and Central African tradition. It involves dancing and singing in a circular pattern. Testifying is another kind of praise. It is telling the story of experiencing God's enlightenment.

59 What is Black Pentecostalism?

Black Pentecostalism is geared toward the Holy Spirit and God's immediate presence. It is high energy. From the beginning, the movement gave rise to diverse values and expressions. They have included social ethics, economic justice, gender equality and contemporary issues.

60 What are the roots of Pentecostalism?

Pentecostalism goes back to the 1906 Azusa Street Revival in Los Angeles. It was led by William Joseph Seymour, a Christian fundamentalist preacher. This series of meetings was characterized by speaking in tongues. It gave rise to Pentecostal and charismatic theologies. Pentecostals believe the Holy Spirit works within people to inform their interpretation of the Bible. The Church of God in Christ came out of the Azusa Street Revival. It is one of the Black Churches and the largest Pentecostal denomination in the United States.

Music

61 What are spirituals?

Spirituals are traditional songs drawn from African American religion and culture. Enslaved people used song as a public channel for private communication among themselves. These songs could be used to express shared sorrow, joy, inspiration, hope and more. People familiar with the tradition and culture understood their meaning. They were passed down through generations in the oral tradition. Some people have strayed from traditional African American spirituals because they originated in slavery. Others, such as James W. Story, a lifelong music educator, maintained these songs are crucial to understanding history. During slavery, "coded escape songs" guided and warned people. For example, the song "Follow the Drinking Gourd" directed people to follow the Big Dipper to navigate North. Spirituals unified and animated the civil rights movement.

62 What are the origins of gospel music?

Black gospel music evolved from spirituals, Christian hymns of the early 19th century and songs of the enslaved. Gospel music came to be around 1930. According to the Library of Congress, "The storefront churches of the northern cities became the key setting for the development of gospel." This music allows for the passionate expression of the church's beliefs. Gospel has long inspired and supported Black Americans' fight for equality.

63 How did hymns, gospel and spirituals evolve?

Dr. Fredara Hadley, an ethnomusicology professor at The Juilliard School, said musical development is a story of chronology and evolving structure. Henry Louis Gates Jr.'s "The Black Church: This Is Our Story, This Is Our Song" quotes Hadley: "The folk spirituals emerge during the period of enslavement. There's an identifiable structure there, but the words are interchangeable. Then we get into hymns. Hymns have this standard verse-chorus structure, and that comes out of European hymnody." She added, "When you get to gospel hymns and gospel, you have the merger of all of those things."

64 What is modern gospel?

Modern gospel is the collision and fusion of modern jazz, hip-hop, blues, rap, pop and traditional gospel. Modern gospel is sometimes seen as a controversial crossover. Dr. Deborah Smith Pollard, professor of English literature and humanities at the University of Michigan-Dearborn says there is no need for conflict. In her book, "When the Church Becomes Your Party," she says modern gospel is valid worship and expands the church's reach. She cites performer scholar Horace C. Boyer. He said: "Many gospel music lovers insist that African American preachers were the first rappers, and that gospel rappers were long overdue." Pollard calls holy hip-hoppers "preachers in disguise," as dedicated as any traditional gospel artist or minister of music to praise and worship.

65 How do sacred and secular music interact?

Henry Louis Gates Jr. writes in "The Black Church: This Is Our Story, This Is Our Song" that they go hand in hand. He describes how Aretha Franklin's singing was always spiritual, even in secular songs. Gates wrote, "Aretha has never left the church, because the church had never left her."

66 How has the church influenced contemporary music?

Aretha Franklin, John Legend and the Winans family are just a few of the artists who started out singing in church. Gospel music often focuses on rhythm and soul which influences today's Black artists. Contemporary church music has become more popular in the present day, and gospel music transcends time. Race records were pivotal in spreading gospel music. Race records are recordings made for Black people by Black people. These records could be bought and sold in stores that catered to Black people, and they gave the genre more exposure.

67 How have artists affected how people view the church?

In their songs and albums, **Beyoncé**, **Chance the Rapper** and **Nicki Minaj** opened the door for listeners and the media to talk about faith. This brings people to explore religion and converse about Christianity and the Black Church. The church has been the cradle for thousands of artists globally. Here is a very partial list.

Yolanda Adams

Ruth Brown

The Rev. Shirley Caesar

Kurt Carr Singers

The Clark Sisters

Merry Clayton

The Rev. James Cleveland

Dorothy Love Coates

Tasha Cobbs Leonard

Sam Cooke

Ricky Dillard

Aretha Franklin

Kirk Franklin

Marvin Gaye

Fred Hammond

The Hawkins Family

Israel Houghton

Mahalia Jackson

Blind Willie Johnson

Gloria Jones

Tamela Mann

Mary Mary

Donnie McClurkin

The Mississippi Mass Choir

Kelly Price

Lou Rawls

Marvin Sapp

Troy Sneed

Cleotha Staples

Angie Stone

Ira Tucker

Albertina Walker

Hezekiah Walker

Dionne Warwick

Maron Williams

Willmer

The Winans Family

Stevie Wonder

Education

68 What role has the church played in education?

When people could be jailed for teaching African Americans to read and write, education found a home in Black Churches. Baptist churches set up schools where African Americans could become literate. Some had to do it in secret. Learning to read the Bible, which people heard in services, was well suited to the Black Church's duality as a spiritual and social institution.

69 What is Sunday school?

Sunday school is church-affiliated Bible study. It teaches youth about scripture, history and life skills. The first Sunday school was started in 1793 in New York City by Katy Ferguson, who had been born into slavery. One of her early influences was Christian scripture. She brought 48 children into her home to educate them. For some people, the best part of Sunday is when young people are gathered before or after service to learn about their faith. According to Progressive National Baptist Connections, Bible study is grouped by ages: "Children's Corner, ages 5-8; Junior Jaunts, ages 9-13; Teenage Travelogues, ages 14-18."

70 Did Black Churches help start Black colleges?

There is a long-standing symbiosis between religion and higher education in the Black community. Many Historically Black Colleges and Universities, called HBCUs, were founded by churches, and the organizations continue to support each other as leadership pipelines. One of the first HBCUs, Augusta Institute, was established in 1867 in the basement of Springfield Baptist Church. Today, it is Morehouse College in Atlanta. In 1872, African Methodist Episcopal pastors founded Paul Quinn College. The U.S. Department of Education certifies 107 HBCUs in 21 states and the Virgin Islands.

71 Does church support for HBCUs continue today?

The Absalom Jones Fund for Episcopal HBCUs has been giving since the 1800s. In 1944, Black Churches were founding partners in the United Negro College Fund. It awards more than $100 million in scholarships to students at more than 1,100 schools each year. Alfred Street Baptist Church, one of the oldest African American congregations in the nation, gives annually. In 2019, it donated $100,000 to Howard University. In 2022, it gave Dillard University $50,000. Other churches also help. The United Methodist Church, which is not a Black Church, supports 11 HBCUs.

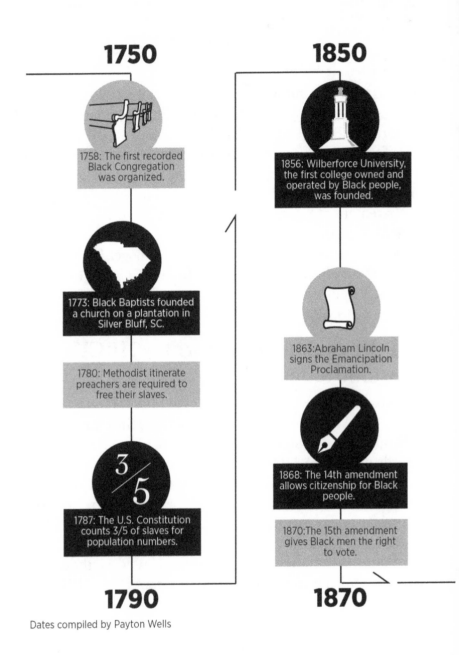

1750

1758: The first recorded Black Congregation was organized.

1773: Black Baptists founded a church on a plantation in Silver Bluff, SC.

1780: Methodist itinerate preachers are required to free their slaves.

3/5

1787: The U.S. Constitution counts 3/5 of slaves for population numbers.

1790

1850

1856: Wilberforce University, the first college owned and operated by Black people, was founded.

1863: Abraham Lincoln signs the Emancipation Proclamation.

1868: The 14th amendment allows citizenship for Black people.

1870: The 15th amendment gives Black men the right to vote.

1870

Dates compiled by Payton Wells

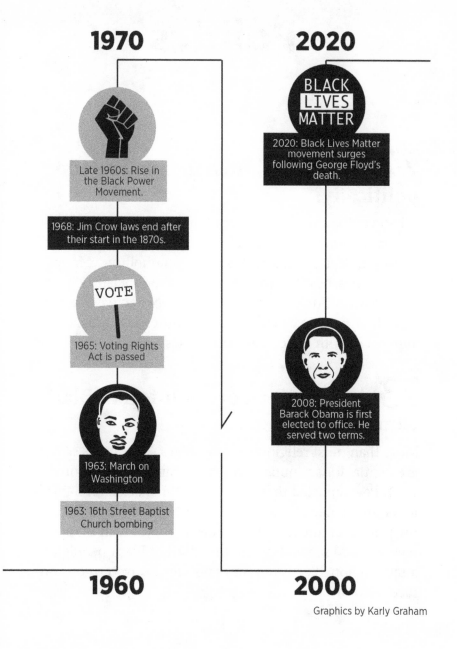

1970

Late 1960s: Rise in the Black Power Movement.

1968: Jim Crow laws end after their start in the 1870s.

VOTE

1965: Voting Rights Act is passed

1963: March on Washington

1963: 16th Street Baptist Church bombing

1960

2020

BLACK LIVES MATTER

2020: Black Lives Matter movement surges following George Floyd's death.

2008: President Barack Obama is first elected to office. He served two terms.

2000

Graphics by Karly Graham

Politics

72 Where do church members stand politically?

Whatever their religion, more than 80 percent of African Americans vote as Democrats, according to Pew research. However, African Americans are not monolithic. Many align with issues that are considered to be socially conservative. African Americans, whether active in the church or not, have held national positions with the support of both major political parties.

73 Are pulpits more political in Black Churches?

More than most religious groups, Black Protestants said it is essential for sermons to cover race and immigration. In 2021, Pew reported that almost half the Black churchgoers in its survey had attended Black Protestant churches in the prior year and heard sermons on topics such as race relations and inequality. About a third of Black people who attended non-Black churches said they heard sermons on race relations.

74 What other issues does the church support?

The Black Church Political Action Committees stresses several. They include ending mass incarceration, defending the right to vote, curbing gun violence and equitable treatment of black and brown communities.

75 Has the Black Church launched political careers?

The Black Church is a wellspring of political, educational, operational and financial support. Many politicians learned public speaking growing up in the supportive haven of the church. Some go on to careers in elected or appointed office. Others lead as civil rights activists, educators and theologians. One is Georgia U.S. Senator **Raphael G. Warnock**, senior pastor of Atlanta's Ebenezer Baptist Church. This is where **Dr. Martin Luther King Jr.** was baptized, ordained and was co-pastor with his father. This is the church where Georgia **U.S. Rep. John Lewis**, the son of sharecroppers, was eulogized. In an interview with NBC News, Warnock said Lewis had "wrestled with a call to ministry early in life. But instead of preaching sermons, he became one. That is his legacy. And it is tied to a church with a storied history of faith and freedom making." Others who credit the Black Church for shaping them are former **President Barack Obama, U.S. Sen. Corey Booker** of New Jersey, **U.S. Rep. Barbara Jordan** of Texas, U.S. ambassador to the United Nations **Andrew Young** and presidential candidate **Jesse Jackson**.

76 Does the church encourage voting?

Political engagement is a major issue in the Black Church, as evidenced by its action around the Voting Rights Act of 1965. Many in the church fought personally for it. Churches unite with the NAACP under slogans such as "Souls to the Polls," "AME Voter Alert" and "COGIC Counts." With today's widespread legislation to discourage Black voting rights, the push for voting access has intensified. The Black Church is not alone in exercising political pressure. Several denominations spend millions of dollars a year on lobbying at state and national levels.

Women

77 What part do women play in the Black Church?

Women have been called the backbone of the Black Church and have made up most of its membership for more than a century. Additionally, Pew found Black women were more likely than Black men to stress the importance of religion. Women's roles are often concentrated in social issues and service, even as they wish to do more spiritual and leadership work. Women frequently serve as ushers, greeters, worship leaders, counselors, in nurseries and more. They also serve on the mother's board as longtime church members who mentor younger women and arrange activities for families and children.

78 Does the Black Church ordain women?

It does, but pulpit placement is inequitable. While there is no formal exclusion against female leadership as there is in some churches, women have not held many national roles. Women have been ordained ministers and have preached since the 1800s. However, men held all denominational leadership positions until the 21st century, according to U.S. News and World Report. Pew reports Black Church sermons are less likely than sermons in White Protestant churches to oppose sexism and more likely to stress the importance of male responsibility in family finances.

79 Are roles for women increasing?

Women are preparing to take more top roles in the church. A 2015 report by American Baptist Churches USA found that women were fewer than 10 percent of its senior or solo pastors. However, they held half the positions in the denomination's seminaries. In 2021, the Rev. Dr. Gina Stewart, the first woman president of a major Black Baptist organization, said "There's a shifting taking place."

80 Who is the "first lady" in a Black Church?

The first lady is the wife of the main male preacher or minister. Responsibilities of the first lady in the church have grown in recent years. It is expanding from community outreach to ministry work.

81 What is a church mother, and what is a mother church?

The church mother is frequently the senior woman in the church. She is respected for her experience and wisdom. She prays for members and looks out for them. The other term, mother church, is how one might refer to their home church. Even when a person moves to another city, they might remain connected with their mother church. This can also mean a church that gives a start to others.

82 How have women changed the church?

Black women developed Womanist Theology, a form of feminism that focuses on the perspective and concerns of African American women. The theology was developed by female theologians, historians, scholars, ethicists and Bible scholars. Novelist and social activist Alice Walker coined the term womanist. It looks at both contemporary and historical issues and goes beyond religion to include politics and power.

Traditions

83 What are revivals?

Today's revivals are local events quite smaller than
the awakenings of the 1700s. They are about bringing
members of a church together to hear visiting pastors and
preachers. This exposes members to fresh perspectives and
different styles of preaching and prayer. People feel that
new experiences help revive one's faith.

84 How often do revivals occur?

Revivals usually occur once or twice a year. They generally
consist of a few days or up to a week's worth of guest
speakers, music, reflection and discussion. Some run for a
shorter length of time.

85 What is Vacation Bible School?

Vacation Bible Schools are typically week-long programs
to teach children about Christianity. The programs often
include shows, skits, theater performances, arts and crafts
and other activities to keep the content engaging. Typically,
the programs are held in summer when children are out
of school. VBS, as it is often called, is not specific to Black
Churches.

86 Why is the first Sunday of each month significant?

On first Sundays, the pastor of that church will be in the pulpit. The congregation may be dressier for first Sundays. In some churches, the first Sunday is generally the one in which churchgoers partake in the sacrament of Communion. This does not occur at every service, as it does in some other denominations. Some churches, recognizing that Communion commemorates the Last Supper, will have this in the evening. Many Christian churches worldwide celebrate their unity by observing the first Sunday in October as "World Communion Sunday." This is a different phenomenon but may be incorporated in Black Churches.

87 What does New Year's Eve mean in Black Churches?

Some Black Churches have services this night for people to be together and enter into the new year with hope and gratitude. Years ago, starting on Dec. 31, 1862, some Black Churches held Freedom's Eve. On it, they awaited or commemorated the signing of the Emancipation Proclamation. That had evolved from Watch Night in which some Christian churches recalled Jesus' appeals to his disciples to watch as he prayed the night he was arrested.

88 What is the significance of women's church hats?

Women in all kinds of churches and other circles have worn showy hats for a long time. Today, their use has declined. Hats have been associated with religion, Easter, suffragettes, social groups, the Golden Age and the British royals. In churches, hats evolved from hair coverings for modesty or humility. In the Black Church, hats can be influenced by African tradition and be seen as symbolic crowns of triumph over adversity.

89 How are handheld fans used in Black Churches?

Historically, people in many kinds of churches fan themselves to stay cool. In the Black Church, fans acquire another layer of messages with ads promoting businesses and events. They are cultural, not religious.

Money

90 Do Black Churches tithe?

This word, which means one tenth, has biblical roots. Tithing is to give 10 percent of one's gross income to church causes. The amount is up to the individual. Though it can be encouraged, tithing is not required.

91 How much money do Black Churches collect?

It depends on the size and wealth of the congregation and where it is located. Some churches are extremely wealthy, and some can barely make ends meet. A church is organized as a non-profit institution and reinvests its earnings into the church to ultimately serve the members. That can mean hiring staff, building renovations or expansion, and educational initiatives.

92 What is the prosperity gospel?

Prosperity theology teaches that God wants people to be healthy and wealthy. It teaches that enough faith, positivity and religious giving will bring these signs of God's love. This philosophy is taught by televangelists and some preachers. The prosperity gospel is sometimes accompanied by social conservatism. In The New York Times, Princeton professor of religion and African American Studies Eddie S. Glaude Jr., called it a threat to the Black Church. He wrote, "In Black America, this theology overtakes calls for economic empowerment. Freedom dreams are supplanted by the aspiration to wealth, a theology that suits a vision of capitalism that is devastating our communities and country."

93 How much are pastors paid?

It depends on the church and the size and means of the congregation. Pastors generally take a vow of poverty and receive just enough to make a living. In wealthier areas, pastors of megachurches can make significantly more. Pastors of some small churches must work multiple jobs to make ends meet.

Future

94 Is the Black Church growing?

Like most faiths in the United States, membership seems to be shrinking. In 2007, 16 percent of all Americans surveyed by Pew said they were not affiliated with an organized religion. In late 2021, that percentage had risen to 30 percent. By contrast, 18 percent of Black Americans said they were religiously unaffiliated. Another 3 percent identified as atheist or agnostic.

95 Do religiously unaffiliated Blacks believe in God?

Most Black Americans who identified as unaffiliated said they were spiritually or religiously engaged in a personal manner. Also, many said they believe in a higher power or pray.

96 Is the church losing younger generations?

The generation issue is a problem for most churches in the United States. Pew noted "Black Millennials and members of Generation Z are less likely to rely on prayer, less likely to have grown up in Black Churches and less likely to say religion is an important part of their lives."

97 How is the church reaching out to young people?

Most churches have always had programming directed to youth. The Black church, like all institutions, needs and welcomes the energy of young people. Some see this as a survival issue and are trying different strategies. Many Sunday school activities, youth departments and the young-adult ministries have updated practices. They use technology more. They are trying Bible apps, and pastors are reaching out through smartphones and social media.

98 Has the internet affected the church?

Many Black Churches offered televised and streaming services even before the COVID-19 pandemic hit in 2020. Online offerings have since grown. It remains to be seen whether people will substitute online services for in-person attendance. Issues will include whether a decrease in personal attendance hurts or helps finances and membership. So far, on-line and in-person options seem to be complementary. Some people appreciate the opportunity to attend a variety of services remotely.

Likelihood to attend predominantly Black congregations by age

Of Black Americans who attend at least a few religious services a year, a majority go to predominantly Black congregations. However, younger Black adults are less likely to.

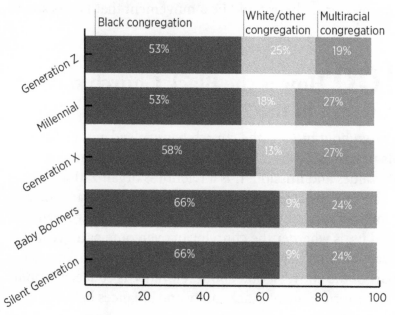

Birth years:
Generation Z, 1997-2012;
Millennial: 1981-1996;
Generation X: 1965-1980;
Baby Boomers: 1946-1964;
Silent Generation: 1928-1945;
A small number of members of the Greatest Generation (born before 1928) were added to the Silent Generation figures. Unanswered responses were omitted.

Source: Pew Research Center and World Religion Database   Graphic by Karly Graham

99 Do worship styles retain people?

This seems to be important. More than half the Protestants in Black congregations told Pew the services they attend are spontaneous, expressive and feature Pentecostal practices such as speaking in tongues. This was more than twice the number of people who reported such experiences in White and other Protestant churches or Black Catholic churches. Given that Black Churches have different atmospheres, there could be a movement that favors some churches.

100 How is the Black Church staying relevant in the 21st century?

Throughout history, the church has evolved and updated its practices, even in the face of persecution, to maintain its values and mission. It is a relentless organization that adapts to obstacles and operates as a safe haven to worship God and serve the community. One challenge, women told us, is whether the church can overcome patriarchal practices that have limited their role and voices. Another part of the conversation about relevance is concerns about the historic issue of Black safety and alliances between the Black Church and Black Lives Matter.

For Discussion and Reflection

1. The Black Church has been referred to as sociological shorthand, an umbrella term for separate denominations with shared religious and social missions. Are there other denominations with close cousins or branches within faiths that are quite similar to different streams of their primary religious identity? Are they encompassed by a shorthand name? Does the U.S. Black Christian church seem to be a unique arrangement?

2. Many churches are a nexus of faith and culture. The Black Church is described as one in which people found ways to make Christianity their own and infused it with African spirituality and traditions. How does this happen in other religions?

3. The crossover and tug-of-war between sacred and secular Black music can be controversial. Does bringing church music and performers into secular contexts debase spiritual music? Does it exploit sacramental music for commercial gain? Or can it be a bridge to God from the secular world? Can the two co-exist? Can they strengthen each other?

4. Souls to the polls, the Black Lives Matter movement and other campaigns demonstrate political activism

in the Black Church. This is nothing new. These churches were center stage in the fight for civil and voting rights more than 60 years ago. So, here's an issue: In a society where religious freedom exempts churches from paying taxes to the government, is it OK that churches try to influence what the government does? Do politics have a place in the pulpit? Do most or all churches do this?

5. Unlike Catholicism and some other religions, Black Christian denominations do not bar women from being ordained. In fact, women have long done much of the churches' work. However, they did not achieve key leadership positions until this century. If more women ascend to leadership, how might the church change? Could this influence other churches?

6. W. E. B. Du Bois wrote that "The Preacher is the most unique personality developed by the Negro on American soil. A leader, a politician, an orator, a 'boss,' an intriguer, an idealist ..." When you consider church membership for yourself, how important is the leader's message and messaging in your decision? Can church leaders be too strong for you, going over the top and eclipsing the message? Can they be too mild?

7. Is congregational engagement in services important to you? Does it deepen your experience to be with people who are actively engaged? Does it pull you in or push you out? Do you feel tension in choosing among churches that share foundational faith values but that offer praise in different ways?

8. Houses of worship are widely regarded as sanctuaries. People have sought refuge in them during wartime and in peace, to avoid arrest and to protest the demolition of communities. But owing in part to their origins as refuges from enslavement, Black Churches take the meaning of sanctuary to a higher level. Because they are seen as safe harbors, they have been targeted by people wishing to strike at the heart of the community. This is different. Do Black Churches require a higher level of protection?

9. A number of historians have said Black Churches have taken on more social and civic responsibilities than is expected of other churches. Does having both spiritual and social missions buoy churches or burden them? Does this dilute church resources or build them up? Should more churches play a larger role in the social sphere?

10. Professor Curtis J. Evans is a University of Chicago Divinity School historian of American religions. He has asked whether the term "Black Church" should be retired. He maintains, "Our time and the complex nature of Black religious life demand a more nuanced and richer rubric than 'the Black Church.' Perhaps some are right that the time for a moratorium on the term has come." He cites the diversity and complexity of the religion. Blacks attend White churches; Whites attend Black Churches and many religious Blacks are not Christian. To newcomers, the term can be confusing. Is it still meaningful? Evans does not propose an alternative but wants people to understand the complexity of the church.

11. The number of Americans who belong to organized religions is declining. Almost all organized religions are losing members, and some try to recruit from one another. Black Churches are losing members, too. What elements of the Black Church's nature and purpose could help it hold or attract members?

12. Music is rooted in the traditions and preaching of the Black Church. It is both a release from sorrow and euphoric praise. Many churches have choir directors, of course, but Black Churches also have ministers of music, musical praise breaks and spirit dancers, as well. Successful pastors pay close attention to these parts of worship. Would you like to see more music in your worship?

Bibliography

Adams Jr., Vaughan L. *The Modern Church Negro: Addressing the Black Community and Christianity.* Fulton: LaBoo Publishing Enterprise. 2021.

Coates, Ta-Nehisi. *Between the World and Me.* London: One World. 2015.

Cone, James H., introduction by Cornel West. *Black Theology and Black Power.* New York City: Orbis. 2019.

Cone, James H. *A Black Theology of Liberation: 50th Anniversary Edition.* New York City: Orbis Books. 2020.

Du Bois, W. E. B., Henry Louis Gates Jr., et al. *Black Folk Then and Now (The Oxford W. E. B. Du Bois): An Essay in the History and Sociology of the Negro Race.* Oxford: Oxford University Press. 2014.

Du Bois, W. E. B. *The Negro Church.* Eugene: Cascade Books. 2011.

Dyson, Michael Eric. *Tears We Cannot Stop: A Sermon to White America.* New York City: St. Martin's Griffin. 2021.

Evans, Curtis J. *The Burden of Black Religion.* Oxford: Oxford University Press. 2008.

Fitts, LeRoy. *A History of Black Baptists.* Nashville: Broadman Press. 1985

Franklin, C. L. (author) and Jeff Todd Titon (editor). *Give Me This Mountain: Life History and Selected Sermons.* Bloomington: University of Indiana Press. 1989.

Frazier, Franklin E., with Eric C. Lincoln. *The Negro Church in America/ The Black Church Since Frazier*. New York City: Schocken Books. 1974.

Gates Jr., Henry Louis. *The Black Church: This Is Our Story, This Is Our Song*. (Accompanies PBS documentary: https://www.pbs.org/show/black-church/ New York City: Penguin Press. 2021.

Gault, Erika D. *Networking the Black Church: Digital Black Christians and Hip Hop*. New York City: NYU Press. 2022.

Hannah-Jones, Nikole. *The 1619 Project: A New Origin Story*. London: One World. 2021.

Higginbotham, Evelyn Brooks. *Righteous Discontent: The Women's Movement in the Black Baptist Church, 1880-1920 (revised)*. Cambridge: Harvard University Press. 1994.

hooks, bell and Cornel West. *Breaking Bread: Insurgent Black Intellectual Life*. Oxfordshire: Routledge. 2016.

Hopkins, Dwight N. *Down, Up, and Over: Slave Religion and Black Theology*. Minneapolis: Fortress Press. 1999.

Indiana University African American Choral Ensemble. *Music of the Black Church*. New York City: Public Broadcasting Service. 2020. https://www.pbs.org/video/amen-music-of-the-black-church-mjpdrd/

Jones, Alisha Lola. *Flaming? The Peculiar Theopolitics of Fire and Desire in Black Male Gospel Performance*. Oxford: Oxford University Press. 2020.

Kendi, Ibram X. and Keisha N. Blain (eds.). *Four Hundred Souls: A Community History of African America, 1619-2019*. London: One World. 2021.

Lewis, John. *Carry On: Reflections for a New Generation*. New York City: Grand Central Publishing. 2021.

Lincoln, C. Eric and Lawrence H. Mamiya. *The Black Church in the African American Experience*. Durham: Duke University Press Books. 1990.

Meacham, Jon with afterword by John Lewis. *His Truth Is Marching On: John Lewis and the Power of Hope*. New York City: Random House. 2020.

Mitchell, Henry H. *Black Church Beginnings: The Long-Hidden Realities of the First Years*. Grand Rapids: Wm. B. Eerdmans. 2004.

Paris, Peter J. *The Social Teaching of the Black Churches*. Philadelphia: Fortress Press. 1985.

Pierce, Yolanda. *In My Grandmother's House: Black Women, Faith and the Stories We Inherit*. New York City: Broadleaf Books. 2021.

Pinn, Anthony B. *The Black Church in the Post Civil Rights Era*. New York City: Orbis Books. 2002.

Pollard, Deborah Smith. *When the Church Becomes Your Party: Contemporary Gospel Music*. Detroit: Wayne State University Press. 2008.

Raboteau, Albert J. *Slave Religion: The "Invisible Institution" in the Antebellum South (updated edition)*. Oxford: Oxford University Press. 2004.

Sampson, Freda G. and the Rev. Dr. Jeremiah A. Wright. *"I Think I Said Something ..." The Life, Legacy & Ministry of Rev. Dr. Frederick G. Sampson, II*. London: Vision Publishing. 2018.

Sharpton, Al. *Rise Up: Confronting a Country at the Crossroads*. New York City: Hanover Square Press. 2020.

Thomas, Todne. *Kincraft: The Making of Black Evangelical Sociality*. Durham: Duke University Press. 2021.

Walker, Alice. *In Search of Our Mothers' Gardens: Womanist Prose*. Boston: Houghton Mifflin Harcourt Publishing Company. 1983.

Warnock, Raphael G. *The Divided Mind of the Black Church: Theology, Piety, and Public Witness.* New York City: NYU Press. 2013.

West, Cornel. *Keeping Faith: Philosophy and Race in America.* Oxfordshire: Routledge. 2008.

Wiggins, Daphne C. *Righteous Content: Black Women's Perspectives of Church and Faith.* New York City: NYU Press. 2006.

Wilmore, Gayraud S. and James H. Cone. *Black Theology: A Documentary History, 1966-1979.* New York City: Orbis Books. 1979.

Denominational websites

African Methodist Episcopal Church: ame-church.com

African Methodist Episcopal Zion Church: amez.org

Christian Methodist Episcopal Church: thecmechurch.org

National Baptist Convention, USA, Inc.: nationalbaptist.com

Church of God in Christ: cogic.org

National Baptist Convention of America International, Inc.: nbcainc.com

Progressive National Baptist Convention, Inc.: pnbc.org

Our Story

The 100 Questions and Answers series springs from the idea that good journalism should increase cross-cultural competence and understanding. Most of our guides are created by Michigan State University journalism students.

We use journalistic interviews to surface the simple, everyday questions that people have about each other but might be afraid to ask. We use research and reporting to get the answers and then put them where people can find them, read them and learn about each other.

These cultural competence guides are meant to be conversation starters. We want people to use these guides to get some baseline understanding and to feel comfortable asking more questions. We put a resources section in every guide we make and we arrange community conversations. While the guides can answer questions in private, they are meant to spark discussions.

Making these has taught us that people are not that different from each other. People share more similarities than differences. We all want the same things for ourselves and for our families. We want to be accepted, respected and understood.

Please email your thoughts and suggestions to series editor Joe Grimm at joe.grimm@gmail.com, at the Michigan State University School of Journalism.

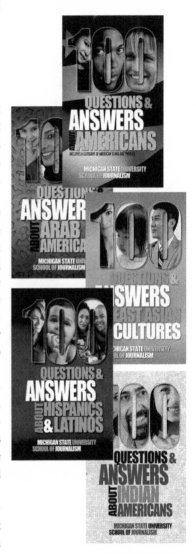

Related Books

100 Questions and Answers About Americans
Michigan State University School of Journalism, 2013

This guide answers some of the first questions asked by newcomers to the United States. Questions represent dozens of nationalities coming from Africa, Asia, Australia, Europe and North and South America. Good for international students, guests and new immigrants.

ISBN: 978-1-939880-20-8

100 Questions and Answers About Arab Americans
Michigan State University School of Journalism, 2014

The terror attacks of Sept. 11, 2001, propelled these Americans into a difficult position where they are victimized twice. The guide addresses stereotypes, bias and misinformation. Key subjects are origins, religion, language and customs. A map shows places of national origin.

ISBN: 978-1-939880-56-7

100 Questions and Answers About East Asian Cultures
Michigan State University School of Journalism, 2014

Large university enrollments from Asia prompted this guide as an aid for understanding cultural differences. The focus is on people from China, Japan, Korea and Taiwan and includes Mongolia, Hong Kong and Macau. The guide includes history, language, values, religion, foods and more.

ISBN: 978-939880-50-5

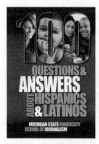

100 Questions and Answers About Hispanics & Latinos
Michigan State University School of Journalism, 2014

This group became the largest ethnic minority in the United States in 2014 and this guide answers many of the basic questions about it. Questions were suggested by Hispanics and Latinos. Includes maps and charts on origin and size of various Hispanic populations.

ISBN: 978-1-939880-44-4

Print and ebooks available on Amazon.com and other retailers.

Related Books

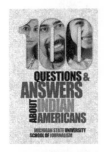

100 Questions and Answers About Indian Americans
Michigan State University School of Journalism, 2013

In answering questions about Indian Americans, this guide also addresses Pakistanis, Bangladeshis and others from South Asia. The guide covers religion, issues of history, colonization and national partitioning, offshoring and immigration, income, education, language and family.

ISBN: 978-1-939880-00-0 m

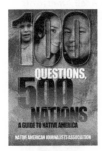

100 Questions, 500 Nations: A Guide to Native America
Michigan State University School of Journalism, 2014

This guide was created in partnership with the Native American Journalists Association. The guide covers tribal sovereignty, treaties and gaming, in addition to answers about population, religion, U.S. policies and politics. The guide includes the list of federally recognized tribes.

ISBN: 978-1-939880-38-3

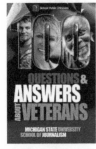

100 Questions and Answers About Veterans
Michigan State University School of Journalism, 2015

This guide treats the more than 20 million U.S. military veterans as a cultural group with distinctive training, experiences and jargon. Graphics depict attitudes, adjustment challenges, rank, income and demographics. Includes six video interviews by Detroit Public Television.

ISBN: 978-1-942011-00-2

100 Questions and Answers About American Jews
Michigan State University School of Journalism, 2016

We begin by asking and answering what it means to be Jewish in America. The answers to these wide-ranging, base-level questions will ground most people and set them up for meaningful conversations with Jewish acquaintances.

ISBN: 978-1-942011-22-4

news.jrn.msu.edu/culturalcompetence

Related Books

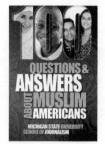

100 Questions and Answers About Muslim Americans
Michigan State University School of Journalism, 2014

This guide was done at a time of rising intolerance in the United States toward Muslims. The guide describes the presence of this religious group around the world and inside the United States. It includes audio on how to pronounce some basic Muslim words.

ISBN: 978-1-939880-79-6

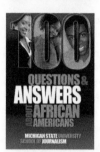

100 Questions and Answers About African Americans
Michigan State University School of Journalism, 2016

Learn about the racial issues that W.E.B. DuBois said in 1900 would be the big challenge for the 20th century. This guide explores Black and African American identity, history, language, contributions and more. Learn more about current issues in American cities and campuses.

ISBN: 978-1-942011-19-4

100 Questions and Answers About Immigrants to the U.S.
Michigan State University School of Journalism, 2016

This simple, introductory guide answers 100 of the basic questions people ask about U.S. immigrants and immigration in everyday conversation. It has answers about identity, language, religion, culture, customs, social norms, economics, politics, education, work, families and food.

ISBN: 978-1-934879-63-4

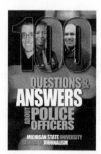

100 Questions and Answers about Police Officers
Michigan State University School of Journalism, 2018

This simple, introductory guide answers 100 of the basic questions people ask about police officers, sheriff's deputies, public safety officers and tribal police. It focuses on policing at the local level, where procedures vary from coast to coast. The guide includes a resource about traffic stops.

ISBN: 978-1-64180-013-6

Print and ebooks available on Amazon.com and other retailers.

Related Books

100 Questions and Answers About Gender Identity
Michigan State University School of Journalism, 2017

The guide is written for anyone who wants quick answers to basic, introductory questions about transgender people. It is a starting point people who want to get a fast grounding in the facts.

ISBN: 978-1-641800-02-0

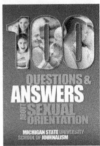

100 Questions and Answers About Sexual Orientation
Michigan State University School of Journalism, 2018

This clear, introductory guide answers 100 of the basic questions people ask about people who are lesbian, gay, bisexual or who have other sexual orientations. The questions come from interviews with people who say these are issues they frequently get asked about or wish people knew more about.

ISBN: 978-1-641800-27-3

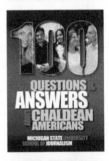

100 Questions and Answers About Chaldean Americans
Michigan State University School of Journalism, 2019

This guide has sections on identity, language, religion, culture, customs, social norms, economics, politics, education, work, families and food. It is written for those who want authoritative answers to basic, questions about this immigrant group from Iraq.

ISBN: 978-1-934879-63-4

100 Questions and Answers About Gen X Plus
100 Questions and Answers About Millennials
Michigan State University School of Journalism, 2019

This is a double guide in the Bias Busters series. It is written for those who want authoritative answers about these important generations and how we all work together.

ISBN: 978-1-641800-47-1

Related Books

True Border: 100 Questions and Answers About the U.S.-Mexico Frontera
Borderzine: Reporting Across Fronteras, 2020

This guide was developed by the University of Texas/Borderzine for the Bias Busters cultural competence series. The guide is written for people who want authoritative answers about the U.S.-Mexico border region and get up to speed quickly on this important topic.

ISBN: 978-1-641800-60-0

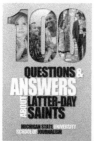

100 Questions and Answers About Latter-day Saints
Michigan State University School of Journalism, 2020

This guide is written for those who want authoritative answers to basic questions about the Latter-day Saints faith. It relies extensively on the Church of Jesus Christ of Latter-day Saints writings and suggests resources for greater depth.

ISBN: 978-1-641800-90-7

100 Questions and Answers About Sikh Americans
Michigan State University School of Journalism, 2022

Sikhism is the fifth largest religion in the world. It is a young religion, having been founded in 1469. It has been in the United States for almost 150 years, but is still relatively unknown. The questions in this guide were created by interviewing Sikhs and asking them what they wish people knew about Sikhs and their religion.

ISBN: 978-1-641801-43-0

Print and ebooks available on Amazon.com and other retailers.

CPSIA information can be obtained
at www.ICGtesting.com
Printed in the USA
LVHW101227150223
739407LV00004B/18